EMPOWERHER
EMPOWERHIM 2

Positive Affirmations for Setting &
Accomplishing Goals

Keshawn Harris

Contents

A Positive Mindset Matters

Mindset matters most. It is important to take care of your mind as well as your body. A positive - mindset is the key to success and living a good life.

However, despite of all the challenges and difficult times you have faced, having a positive mindset can produce outstanding results in your life.

If you look at all the successful people out there, many of them have one thing in common. They witnessed challenging situations.

In challenging situations, you must maintain a positive mindset. A positive mindset will allow you to persist through hardship, find better solutions and help you grow through what you go through. In fact, when tough times arrive, we may be forced to rearrange our plans, living status and priorities. But when you transform your mind you will look at your situation different. A positive mindset will search for light in the darkest tunnel, opportunity to grow through obstacles, turn pain into power and look at setbacks as steppingstones.

As hard as it is sometimes, you must reject those negative thoughts.

However, there are many practical things you can do to stop negative thinking pattern. You can overcome negative thinking by saying affirmations daily. Saying affirmations will reshape your thinking.

If you completed Empower Her this is the next step in your empowerment evolution. You must be consistent with saying your affirmations. This mean using positive sentences 3-5 times a day, repeat to yourself to build up your belief in the subconscious mind. You can always revert to the book EmpowerHer to gain a better understanding of affirmations.

Using the tips and exercises from EmpowerHer will help you to continue growing.

I am so excited were growing together. Now that were in the growth process and gaining a positive mindset it's time to set goals and be more consistent with taking the right steps to accomplish them. Congratulations, you're already ahead of the majority!

A positive mindset will give you the highest probability of reaching your goals.

Without a positive mindset and the drive to want to achieve your goals, you can guarantee you'll fail. Failure is not a good feeling, but it's not the end. We should learn from mistakes and failure. When you learn from mistakes and failures it's a part of a learning process of life. We are constantly learning and developing daily. Don't stop learning or earning. It's time to think big and push yourself out of your comfort zone. It's time to turn dreams into reality.... Think about those routine, subconscious things that could be hindering and anchoring your progress. For example:

late night eating when your goal is to lose weight. Be honest with yourself! You will never lose weight eating late at night.

You must have self-discipline when setting goals. Be honest with yourself, make sacrifices and set realistic goals.

To lose weight you must eliminate bad habits. You must eat fewer calories or burn more calories than you need. Take it slow. Don't allow your habits to sabotage your weight loss. Set small goals, it's smart to aim for losing 1 or 2 pounds a week. Set realistic goals and track your process

Setting your goals might be challenging, I know this book will empower you to unlearn bad habit, make a commitment to discipline yourself, be consistent and make sacrifices through the process.

List all beliefs, facts and habits that are ceasing you from giving your all to your goal / goals right now. Make a list and set realistic goals that will help you and guide you to your long-term goal.

Make your list and work on those bad habits. Greatness takes time. Let's start this process together.

Ask yourself ....

Do I want more? Am I where I want to be in life? If you're answers are yes and no, let's make a change starting today. It is time to make life changes.

Repeat:

- ❖ *I Will achieve my goals.*
- ❖ *No one / nothing will stop me.*
- ❖ *I'm eliminating bad habits*
- ❖ *My life will change for better.*
- ❖ *I am honest with myself*
- ❖ *I am dedicated*
- ❖ *I am a conqueror*
- ❖ *I am self-motivated*

PUSH YOURSELF BECAUSE NO ONE ELSE IS GOING TO DO IT FOR YOU!

#SelfMOTIVATION

Motivation is an important factor in accomplishing your goal. It builds determination. It is important to find what motivates you to achieve your goals. Motivation give you the energy that drives you to accomplish your goals, and it's necessary for any type of success.... Motivation is the energy that keeps you from giving up and to keep trying every time you feel like giving up.

It is both possible and necessary to regain lost motivation, and it's easier than you think! You can take simple steps to stay enthusiastic and committed every step of the way until you achieve your worthwhile goal.

Get motivated and achieve your goals

- ❖ *Know your goal*
- ❖ *Know the purpose of why your setting this goal*
- ❖ *Create clear vision*
- ❖ *Produce a plan*
- ❖ *PRAY over & through your plan*
- ❖ *Declare Positive affirmations*
- ❖ *Approach task in new ways*
- ❖ *Get organized*
- ❖ *Set deadlines*
- ❖ *Accept mistakes / failure*
- ❖ *Compete with yourself*
- ❖ *Finds what motivate you*
- ❖ *Let's get motivated and have fun through the process.*

Don't Tell People Your Dreams Show Them!

6

Goal Digger

"goal digger" refers a woman or man who seeks to better her or his life and the lives of those around them. They do not use people for personal materialistic gain. In fact, you want to surround yourself with goal diggers because they often serve as a means of inspiration.

Setting Goals

"Setting Goals" Identifying something that you want to accomplish and establishing measurable goals and timeframes.

A prayer + an action plan = achieved goal

Invite God into your goal setting process with prayer and patience allow him to instruct you.

When we invite god in our hearts, spirits and mind, we have gods promise to help and instruct us to attain the desires of our hearts.

Psalm 37:4 delight yourself in the lord, and he will give you the desires of your heart.

When setting goals, you must consider what you want to achieve and then commit to it. Be clear and well defined. Set smart, realistic, measurable and attainable goals. Write it down, visualize your goal, create a list of pros and cons and find what motivate you. Speak greatness over yourself, encourage yourself. Repeat your daily affirmation. Make an action plan and stick with it. Set time bound goals. Set a deadline for your goal. Goals must have a clearly defined time frame including the start date and the target date for your completion.

You will rise your self - confidence, as you recognize your own strength and ability to carry out the goals you have set.

You should be already and set to write down your goals the steps and strategies you will need to get there. In order to accomplish the goal, you must plan your attack.

Don't despise small beginnings. Every step matters!

Dream big and don't forget all great things come with hard work and in time.

Lastly, pat yourself on the back for all the small steps you take to get to your dream! Without them, you can't get to where you are destined to go!

Let's start planning and break it down into component parts of goals, strategies, objectives, and tactics.

- ❖ *GOAL — A broad primary outcome.*
- ❖ *STRATEGY — The approach you take to achieve a goal.*
- ❖ *OBJECTIVE — A measurable step you take to achieve a strategy.*
- ❖ *TACTIC — A tool you use in pursuing an objective aligned with your strategy.*
- ❖ *Goals*

Goal #1

3 Strategies to achieve goal

_____

_____

_____

_____

_____

What is the benefit of this goal?

_____

_____

_____

_____

What steps are needed to achieve this goal?

_____

Who can help achieve this goal?

5 tactics for completing each strategy

_____

_____

_____

I will achieve this goal by

_____

_____

_____

_____

_____

You've set your goal now what?

We always set goals with the best of intentions, but it's so easy to get distracted. Life situations and challenges may get in the way or we may lose that inspiration that inspired us to get started and slowly but surely, we land back at square one. We have the stay motivated and work at it every day to gain a great benefit. Being consistent is the best way to achieve your goals and will also help you hit those major milestones.

Consistent means to be dedicated to completing your goal. To be engaged without distractions. It requires commitment.

CONSISTENCY AND ACTION!

Consistency and action:

Consistency and action are the most important habits for success. If you have a great plan, you need to take action and execute.

With your goals and your game plan, the next step to get closer to your goal is consistency and action. Let's make SUCCESS a habit. We are what we repeatedly do.

CONSISTENT EFFORTS DAILY RESULT IN MASSIVE SUCCESS

Affirmations:

I will stay Motivated

I visualize myself achieving it

I will make sacrifices

I will create accountability

I will be consistent

I will take brakes as needed.

I will not allow distractions to anchor me

I will prep for success.

I Will Speak Positive Through the process

I Will Achieve My Goals

Make a list of your accomplishments to Keep you inspired to achieve your goals!

Accomplishments

_____

_____

_____

_____

_____

_____

_____

_____

_____

Stick to Your Goal and Plan

Setting goals is one thing but acting and sticking to it is another. Let's turn plans into reality.

Here are a few tips to increase your chances of successfully following your plans

1. Write it down.
2. Track Progress...
3. Set Deadlines.
4. Reward yourself.
5. Have an accountability partner.

Be consistent, make your goal and plan clear.

- Dream big,
- Be descriptive,
- Be specific, • Be realistic.

Track Your Progress...

Monitor development of your goal and plan.

- Write down all and stay motivated.
- If you have a setback, refocus and keep going

- Edit your plan.

Set Deadlines.

Use time wisely. Time yourself to make sure you don't lack with completing goals.

- Make realistic timelines and stick to it.
- If you don't achieve a specific task within the timeline, adjust the deadline.
- Planning is key to achieving things in a timely manner.

Reward yourself.

Working toward your goals is hard work. Think of small rewards to give yourself when you accomplish something big or small. These bonuses will help you stay motivated.

- Find things you enjoy doing to relax, this will help you to stay focused.
- Remember, you are your biggest supporter and cheerleader.
- Don't reward yourself too big now because you need that big thing when you reach the finish line!

Have an accountability partner.

It's important to not try to complete your goals alone. Find a accountability partner (one or two people) who will help you stick to your goal and plan. Your accountability partner does not have to be one of your close friends. This can be a friend, a life coach, your classmate, coworker, praying partner, etc.

- accountability partner can help you
- identify your weaknesses, make plans to overcome them and hold you accountable for making progress.
- •Your partner will remind you of deadlines and give you encouragement when you face setbacks.
- •Being accountable to something means that you are willing to make commitments and be responsible for your own actions. This promotes trust between you and the people around you. Surround yourself around people who push you and encourage you to evolve.

One of many challenges is maintaining positivity in a world that is always focused on negativity. The news, social media, radio, television shows we watch, our communities, on the job, hair salon and barber shop gossip, pretty much everywhere else is filled with terrible events and negative talk.

The truth of this matter is you can't have a life of positivity while spending a lot of time with people who tearing you down.

The good news is that there is a simple solution! Surround yourself with positive, uplifting people.

"When I started eliminating bad habits. I changed the places I used to go, the people I associated with and things I did that served me no good.

My mindset changed when I started rejecting negative thoughts. I served an eviction notice the critic voice that lived inside of my mind. I learned the importance of speaking and expecting great things for myself. I now practice and speak positive affirmations on a day to day basis. I surround myself with more inspiring people who encourage and uplift me, I'm on a journey that separates me from places and things that don't contribute to my development or happiness.

It's easier said than done. It's a constant fight. I must do an ongoing self-evaluation. Evaluating me.

It is a plus to have an accountability partner. The road to success can be lonely. Surround yourself with the right company. Someone that's not afraid to evaluate you and keep you on track. Accountability means answering or accounting for your actions and results constantly pushing and encouraging each other.

Do you have an accountability partner?

Its ok if your answer is yes or no. we all need a mentor or accountability partner to help you identify your weakness, make plans to overcome them and grow to help you, take responsibility and actions to turn your dreams into reality, be happy and live your best life.

I'm so excited. We are growing together. You have an accountability partner in me.

It's time to accomplish more

I mentor a group of women. I do my best to keep a positive attitude whenever we are together. I can't allow life challenges to change my perspective or attitude. I must keep it all together, because our energy is contagious. It can encourage or discourage someone. Do you know the women I mentor run longer and with confidence when they are encouraged? They accomplish more than they thought they would. Why? because they are encouraged to believe they can and so will you!

If I was to discourage them with negative vibes and attitude it would distract them and slow them all the way down. It is important to give positive vibes, attitudes and set a positive tone even when life challenges hit us. Be a great motivation, inspire someone and be inspired. Having an accountability partner or a mentor can be a great benefit with the right connection. it's a two-way street, both partners must put positive vibes in the atmosphere and have a great connection.

As a mentor if I tell you that you can do more and your constantly speaking negative and not putting your best foot forward towards being great or accomplishing your goals. Eventually I'll disconnect. I can't afford to allow you to drain me. We can't allow people to drain us or drag us down with their negativity. We must connect with people that's ready to evolve. Make sure your accountability partner or anyone your allowing in your atmosphere is honorable, consistent, dedicated and have your best interests. If not it's ok to disconnect from people who are not consistent, honorable or ready to grow, excellent. We must protect our peace and destiny throughout this process. Make sure the people you connect with don't break you but make you. If not it's ok to love them from a distance. No distractions allowed.

Accountability partners should not be a distraction. Your partner should be a great inspiration help you keep commitment and hold you accountable for your actions.

Choose your accountability partner wisely.
It's time to make wise decisions, progress and do more!

Ready? Set GROW!

List Accountability Partners

Benefits to Having Accountability

You can do whatever you want to do and be whoever you want to become.

1. Accountability helps your performance
2. Accountability helps measure your success
3. Accountability Keeps you motivated
4. Accountability Help you stay grounded
5. Accountability Validate your thoughts and ideas
6. Accountability will not agree with you all the time
7. Accountability will push you when your lacking
8. Accountability will congratulate you and be happy for your success

Stick to Good Habits and Be Encouraged!

Sticking to good habits can be hard work. Trial and error are a part of the process. Don't declare failure simply because you messed up or because you're having trouble reaching your goals. Instead, use trial and error as an opportunity to grow and to gain knowledge.

- Be Encouraged
- Giving up is not an option

You will never see the end if you give up in the middle
- JOYCE MEYERS

QUITTING IS NOT AN OPTION IF YOU DON'T QUIT YOU WILL FIND A WAY TO MAY IT HAPPEN.

we all get those feelings of doubt, fear and lack of self -confidence. No matter how self- driven you may
 Be, we all face a challenging period. Motivation goes out the window and you feel like giving up. despite of how you may be feeling at that moment you must remind yourself giving up is not an option.

No matter how big the challenge is don't give up when you face discouragement don't give up when you can't control the situation don't give up when the going gets tough don't give up when facing rejection success is not an overnight journey. It takes a lot of sacrifice, effort, challenges and hard work to get to success. So, rather than giving up make a wiser decision. Shift your perspective and grow through the process.

The best views come after The hardest climb

QUESTIONS?
&
ANSWERS

How often do you evaluate yourself, the people around you, your daily activities and the places you may go?

_____

_____

_____

_____

_____

What could you do to improve your position substantially in every aspect?

_____

_____

_____

_____

What could you stop doing right now that is detrimental to your vision and core values, your physical or financial health, relationships and partnerships, or happiness?

Do you feel confident that you can and will achieve your goal?

Let us get to the root of why you want to achieve this goal.

What is your desired result?

What's your strengths?

TO BECOME STRONGER, YOU MUST FIRST FACE YOUR WEAKNESS.

What's Your Weakness?

_____

_____

_____

_____

_____

Here's a few ways you can turn your weakness into strength....

- ❖ Recognize and accept your weaknesses
- ❖ Research and gain knowledge
- ❖ Seek guidance from mentor or an accountability partner
- ❖ Create a strategic improvement plan
- ❖ Be dedicated and follow through with improvement plan
- ❖ Practice makes perfect

To whom much is given, much will be required

Luke 12:48

How can you overcome your fears to achieve your goals?

_____

_____

_____

_____

_____

_____

_____

List Fears & Overcome them

_____

_____

_____

_____

The more benefits you attach to each of your goals, the more likely you will face fears and keep working towards it with all of your efforts.

Let your faith be bigger than your fears
Let's Achieve your goals ....
goal getter
Ready Set goals!

Goal Statement:

_____

_____

_____

_____

What is the benefit of this goal?

What steps are needed to achieve this goal?

Who can help achieve this goal?

Goal #2

3 Strategies to achieve goal

_____

_____

_____

_____

_____

5 tactics for completing each strategy

_____

_____

_____

_____

_____

I will achieve this goal by

_____

_____

_____

_____

_____

Set your goals high, and don't stop till you get there.
- Bo Jackson

Goal Statement:

_____

_____

_____

_____

_____

What is the benefit of this goal?

_____

_____

_____

_____

What steps are needed to achieve this goal?

_____

_____

_____

_____

Who can help achieve this goal?

_____

_____

_____

_____

GOAL#3

3 Strategies to achieve goal

_____

_____

_____

_____

_____

5 Tactics for completing each strategy

_____

_____

_____

_____

_____

I will achieve this goal by

_____

_____

_____

_____

_____

YOUR LIMITATION – ITS ONLY YOUR IMAGINAION.

Goal #4

_____

_____

_____

_____

_____

5 tactics for completing each strategy

_____

_____

_____

_____

_____

I will achieve this goal by

_____

_____

_____

_____

_____

Don't Be afraid. Be Determined.
Be Focused.
Be Hopeful.
Be Empowered.

-Michelle Obama

**THE NUMBER 5 SYMBOLIZE AND REPRESENTS
GOD'S GRACE
GODS GOODNESS AND GOODNESS TO HUMMANITY
GRACE CHANGES EVERYTHING**

**JUST WHEN LIFE TRIES TO OVERWHELM YOU, GODS
GRACE IS THERE TO PICK YOU UP.**

Goal #5

_____

_____

_____

_____

3 Strategies to achieve goal

_____

_____

_____

_____

5 tactics for completing each strategy

I will achieve this goal by

Surround yourself only with people Who are going to take you higher

- Orpah Winfrey

Goal #6

_____

_____

_____

_____

_____

3 Strategies to achieve goal

_____

_____

_____

_____

_____

5 tactics for completing each strategy

_____

_____

_____

_____

_____

I will achieve this goal by

_____

_____

_____

_____

Stay focused, go after your dreams and keep moving toward your goals.
- LL Cool J.

The more time you spend contemplating what you should have done;
You lose valuable time planning what you can and will do. "

— Lil Wayne

STICK THE ORIGINAL PLAN

(MARK YOUR CALENDAR)

Turn Obstacles into Opportunities!

EmpowerHer EmpowerHim 2

MONTH _____   YEAR _____

SUNDAY	MONDAY	TUESDAY	WEDNESDAY	THURSDAY	FRIDAY	SATURDAY

MONTH _____				YEAR _____		
SUNDAY	MONDAY	TUESDAY	WEDNESDAY	THURSDAY	FRIDAY	SATURDAY

It's never too late to start over

MONTH _____				YEAR _____		
SUNDAY	MONDAY	TUESDAY	WEDNESDAY	THURSDAY	FRIDAY	SATURDAY

MONTH _____   YEAR _____

SUNDAY	MONDAY	TUESDAY	WEDNESDAY	THURSDAY	FRIDAY	SATURDAY

"You are never too old or young to set a goal or to dream big''

MONTH _____				YEAR _____		
SUNDAY	MONDAY	TUESDAY	WEDNESDAY	THURSDAY	FRIDAY	SATURDAY

MONTH _____   YEAR _____

SUNDAY	MONDAY	TUESDAY	WEDNESDAY	THURSDAY	FRIDAY	SATURDAY

GREAT THINGS NEVER COME FROM COMFORT ZONES

— KEEDY BLACK

Let's Take NOTES

Take one step of Faith

Every day may not be good but there is good in every day!

Don't be moved by what you see God can do it!

Watch your thoughts, they become words, watch your words, they become actions & actions become habits

Dreams come true every day!

Aspire to inspire before you inspire

Attitude is a little thing that makes a big difference

Humble yourself before the lord and he will exalt you.

For I know the plans I have for you, declares the Lord.
"Plans to Prosper you and not to harm you,
Plans to give you hope and a future

- Jeremiah 29:11

I CAN DO EVERYTHING IN HIM WHO GIVES ME STRENGTH PHILIPPIANS 4:13

The lord is faithful to all his promises and loving toward all he has made. - Psalm 145:13

Depend on the Lord on whatever you do, and your plans will succeed. – Prov. 16:3

No More Procrastinating

Procrastination is simply putting things off - and we've all done it at some stage. It doesn't mean you're lazy or not productive, it just means you may be focusing on some tasks at the expense of others, or maybe you're just having some difficulty getting a particular task started.

Goal setting is at the top of the chart to get put-off. Why? because it's often seen as a non-urgent activity (even though it's extremely important), so effectively self-discipline and managing your time is important for achieving goal setting success.

If you are one that have been a lifelong procrastinator, it's time to stop procrastinating, stop putting things off until deadline, manage your time and discipline yourself

I have been doing a lot of reading and researching about procrastination. I learned a lot during my research. Procrastination Is a delay or postpone action; put off doing something. It is a silent killer.

Procrastination kills your desires, motivations and dreams slowly, without you noticing.

Procrastination kills.

Procrastination kills your productivity.

Procrastination kills your ambition.

Procrastination kills opportunities.

Procrastination suffocates and kills motivation.

Procrastination kills progress.

Procrastination kills the projects you long for most.

Procrastination kills your vision

Procrastination kills your dreams.

Then I learned that

Procrastination is the thief of time.

Here are 3 reasons procrastination is the thief of time:

1. Time never stops, never slows down, is always moving.
2. Once it's gone, it's gone forever.
3. Therefore, time is the one resource that can never be replaced.

If you spend money, you can always get it back.

A lot of distractions, even one small disruption, can be enough to cause you to procrastinate. To avoid these distractions, you must be able to identify them.

Here are 5 things that can distract us on the day to day basis

- Online: social media, checking emails and other things online
- False needs that cause procrastination
- Neglecting yourself and things you need to do, to assist or help someone else with their baggage.
- Lack of time management
- Fear

It's time to put a end to you procrastinating and putting off action on a goal or any other task of yours.

The important question is, "Why?". Why do you procrastinate? And if you know WHY are you procrastinating

Your attitude and behavior will indicate some of the causes of your procrastination.

Most people cannot recognize or identify with their attitude, bad behavior or Procrastination. They always have an excuse for everything. It is important to recognize your behavior have an influence on how you act on particular tasks and which ones you are likely to procrastinate over.

Here are some common causes:

- There are more enjoyable things to do! Or perhaps you're just waiting to be in the right frame of mind for launching into action.

- The tasks is out of your comfort zone

- Lack of knowledge and resources. Most people don't know where to start, particularly if the task is not within their normal skill set or lack resources.

- Fear of failure is the reason many people don't achieve their goals.

- Just can't get started – building up enough momentum to get the ball rolling can take unforeseen effort depending on the task.

You know yourself better than anyone else – are you prone to procrastination? Why? Now, be honest with yourself.

Positive affirmations will empower you to stop procrastination and to take control of your own life and become the productive, successful person you desire to be.

It's time to break the habit of always putting things off. You have told yourself "I'll do it tomorrow" so many times that this has literally became your normal way of thinking. Positive affirmations will help you to reset your mindset and re-write these habitual thought patterns so that taking action, being proactive and getting things done on time becomes a natural part of your lifestyle.

I recommend that you continue to practice positive affirmations at least twice daily, and to activate these affirmations whenever you find yourself slipping into a mode of procrastination or telling yourself "I'll get it done later". Practice makes perfect. Continue to remind yourself, I can't put this one off, read your positive affirmations for stopping procrastination and take control of your life!

Present Tense Affirmations
I act now
I am a doer
I take charge and get things done
I am always moving forward and working on my goals
I work hard first and play later
I always start a project right away
I always get a head start and have plenty of time to complete my work

Others admire that I make things happen now rather than later

I complete projects with plenty of time to spare

Future Tense Affirmations

I am turning into a proactive person

I will stop procrastination and change my life

I will become someone who takes action

I am finding it easier to begin large projects

I will always get started right away, even if I don't feel like it

I am becoming more productive with each passing moment

I am changing into someone who effortlessly gets things done

Natural Affirmations

I love the feeling of getting a head start

It's normal for me to start projects early

Being proactive comes naturally to me

I take action and get things done

Making the best use of my time comes easy to me

I'm the kind of person who always dives straight into my work

I enjoy starting quickly and beating others to the punch

Well, with help from these positive affirmations, this is really possible – they will help you to restructure your mind, to eliminate the negative thoughts which are holding you back and limiting your potential.

So, start using your affirmations and achieve the goals you have set. After all, setting goals is not the hard part, eliminating procrastination, sticking to your goals and achieving them is the challenging part.

It takes planning, focus, perseverance, foresight, dedication, visualization, and hard work to achieve any worthwhile goals. Affirmations help you achieve the focus and visualization parts of reaching your goals.

Side note: Another positive way to improve your life is to read and learn something new every day.

List 10 things that cause you to procrastinate

1. _____

2. _____

3. _____

4. _____

5. _____

6. _____

7. _____

8. _____

9. _____

10. _____

Let's overcome procrastination

Create your own affirmation for each cause you listed above.

(For example:)

Cause	Affirmation
Laziness	I am energetic
Time management	I am always on time

Create 10 Affirmations

1. _____

2. _____

3. _____

4. _____

5. _____

6. _____

7. _____

8. _____

9. _____

10. _____

Set Milestones

Milestones are actions and achievements necessary to make progress toward your goals.

As milestones are reached, you should see progress, assess, new opportunities and make adjustments.

When setting goals, you have to be clear about what you want and setting milestones let you know if you're actually getting there.

It is important to set your milestone, they will motivate you: this means your accomplishments will motivate you to keep climbing to the top, they are important and valuable to you.
Break your goals down and make making accomplishments.

Firstly, you need to break your long-term goal down into short term goals. For example: 40kg weight loss. In the case of weight loss, you might want to focus on dieting, fitness and lifestyle. You'll then break each of these parts down into your short-term goals. Your goals should be Specific, Measurable, Attainable, Realistic and Timely.
A short-term goal for fitness might be to run 6 mile run in 30 minutes. A short-term diet goal might be to eat more vegetables during dinner. Setting short - term goals that's driven and achievable.
These goals should be written down, and or displayed somewhere visible for your daily motivation.
Trust your process and track your progress, it's a great way to retain focus. It gives you the opportunity to pat yourself on the back for your hard work and efforts so far.

This will motivate you through the process to reaching your milestones.

No matter how we structure our goals, it's almost inevitable that we sometimes lose motivation or get too busy.

"Stick To Your Goals"

Make a list of motivations. This list can be a great inspiration when the going gets tough.

When the going gets tough, the tough get going!

What's Your Motivation ?

Make another list of reasons that may stop you from achieving your short-term goals.

For example, you don't want to exercise in the heat, cold or rain, your schedule is too busy, or you haven't got the time to eat healthy Make a list of solutions to your problems: training indoors, prioritizing your time, self-discipline with eating healthy, buying groceries online to save on shopping time, etc.

Make A List of Pros & Cons

Pros	Cons

This information will give you the opportunity to change or reset any unrealistic goals. Reaffirm your decision to set yourself on this path of success.
It's an important to track your progress and ultimately, achievement.

*Success is not a race.
(Be patient)

*Success leads to **success**.
(Trust the process)

 *Success is always a work in progress. (track your progress)

*Success doesn't come to you-you go to it. (press your way through)

SUCCESS!
IT DOSENT HAPPEN OVERNIGHT

Success comes to those who wait and are persistent at what they do.

SUCCESS HAS NO GENDER, AGE, SIZE OR COLOR

SLOW PROCESS IS STILL PROGRESS

TRACKING YOUR PROGRESS

TRACK YOUR PROCESS BIT BY BIT THATS HOW YOU'LL KNOW HOW FAR YOU HAVE CAME.

Recording your goals will help you track them in such a way that you can monitor your strengths, weaknesses, and what steps you should take to improve your journey.

measure your progress so you know what needs to be improved, set targets and reminders, celebrate your milestones, and view your journey. Stay on track and monitor where your time is going every day, so you can be sure to prioritize what matters most in hitting your milestones.

Keep track of and manage your routines, habits and daily goals. Create a to do list to help keep you on track.

Recording your goals, journaling, habit tracking, and tracking your progress most definitely will keep you on the right path.

SUCCESS ISN'T ALWAYS ABOUT GREATNESS ITS ABOUT CONSISTENCY. CONSISTENT HARD WORK LEADS TO SUCCESS. GREATNESS WILL COME.

Consistency is key! It is important to be consistent with your work, writing, "take consistent action every single day of your life." This means that even when you don't feel like doing it do it any way, push yourself, do one small proactive thing that will move you towards your ultimate goal.

Do something today that will make tomorrow better than yesterday.

Make a commitment to yourself, right now, that tomorrow will be a better day, and invest in that belief. You'll be amazed what an impact it has on your outlook.

Stick to your plan and follow through with your daily to do list. Don't Procrastinate. Procrastinating is simply putting things off. Majority of us is gifted when it comes to procrastinating and a few have done it at some stage, even if you're a high-flying executive. It doesn't mean you're not lazy or productive, it just means you may be focusing on some tasks at the expense of others, or maybe you're just experiencing difficulties of getting a particular task started.

With the right mindset, attitude, a solid plan, and the right tools at your disposal, even a challenging day can become manageable. Don't allow one challenging day ruin the rest of your day or week, take action now to make sure tomorrow becomes a better day.

Your present situation is not your final destination
Let your challenging days lead you into better days

Say your affirmations and believe them. Pay full attention to the words you speak and repeat.

For additional power, write your affirmation down as you speak it in the atmosphere. Say your affirmation out loud in a confident voice several times a day. Say them in the morning, throughout your day and before you go to bed at night.

Positive Affirmations for Success:

- I am successful
- I can do it
- I am always on time
- I love to read
- I love learning new things
- I have a positive attitude
- I am a great listener
- I accept constructive criticism
- I make improvements
- I'm getting stronger and wiser

Positive affirmations for personal success:

- Every day I become more successful
- I am successful in my daily life.
- I feel powerful
- I am full of life and good energy
- I am capable and confident
- I learn from my mistakes
- My mistakes are stepping stones to my success
- I love challenges
- I easily find solutions to problems
- I move quickly past roadblocks

Positive affirmations for career success:

- I am an excellent worker
- I am always productive and giving my best effort
- I am experiencing success in my career
- I enjoy working toward future career success
- I have a satisfying job
- I know exactly what I need to do to achieve success in my career
- My work environment is calm and productive

Positive Affirmations for Financial Success

- I am a money magnet
- Money knows my name
- I spend my money wisely
- I am wealthy
- I am financially successful in all my endeavors
- I am getting wealthier each day
- I am living the life
- My dreams are coming true
- I have enough wealth to fulfill my desires

Positive Affirmations for Self-Confidence

- I am beautiful
- I am intelligent
- I am outgoing
- I have a growth mindset
- I have a positive attitude
- I am confident of my future
- I am confident, enthusiastic, and energetic
- I am Love
- I attract loving people

- I attract confident people
- I love change
- I easily adjusting to new people and situations
- I love meeting strangers
- I thrive on self-confidence, knowing that nothing is impossible
- I am outgoing and make friends easily

Positive Affirmations for Mental Health

- I control my mind
- I awake each day with excited.
- I expect great things to come to me
- I am thankful
- I release all stress from my mind and body
- I forgive myself for mistakes and bad decisions I have made
- I observe my emotions without over reacting
- I meditate with joy and without resistance or anxiety
- I reject negative thoughts

Positive Affirmations for Decision Making

- I am patient when making decisions
- I weigh out my options before making decisions
- I make the right decision always
- I receive all advice and feedback with grateful kindness
- I trust myself to make the best decisions

Positive Affirmations for Women

- I am bold and Confident
- I am sure of myself
- I uplift others
- I am a loving daughter, sister and friend

- I see to the needs of those I love
- I am a loving wife and mother,
- I successfully create a loving home environment
- I am a wonderful mother
- My children love and respect me
- I am beautiful
- I am happy
- I am healthy
- I am capable
- I am and kind
- I am constantly learning new things and developing my personality
- I am happy to be a woman
- I am loving
- I am giving and receiving love unconditionally
- I am successful in my chosen career
- I see to the needs of my household with pride and capability

AFFIRMATIONS FOR MEN

- I am bold and confident
- I am sure of myself
- I am outgoing and charismatic
- I am assertive and strong
- I am smart, generous and good at my job
- I am a great provider for my family
- I am the creator of my life
- I am a good person
- People enjoy being around me
- My confidence grows stronger each day
- I love the person I am becoming
- I have great ideas
- I will continue to grow and learn

Affirmations For ENCOURAGEMENT

- I' m close to making my dreams come true
- I am living the life I always wanted
- I am strong
- I am courageous
- I am independent
- I learn from any challenges I encounter
- I strongly believe in my abilities.
- I am worthy of happiness
- I am wealth
- I am living in peace
- I am grateful for the abundance I have

How often have you set a new goal and felt 'this is the one! and to look back a few weeks or months later and trying to figure out where all the motivation you had went?

You be lit and filled with excitement when you first visualize yourself pursuing a new goal. As time pass your excitement starts to fade away as the hard work of pursuing your goal kicks in.

We all know that you have to put in work for anything that is worth having. Nothing worthwhile comes without work, but somehow fear creeps in and tell you your goal can be incredibly hard to accomplish.

All of a sudden, it doesn't feel as exciting now. You started making excuses to yourself in case you fail, or you can't really recall why you were so excited in the first place.

Remember you had good reasons to follow your goal. You need to recall why you set the goal those reasons not just logically but with your heart and your feelings.

Stay loyal to your goals even when it seems difficult, you will get the right reward at the right time. Keep pushing and use your affirmations to help you stay motivated and focused. Use them regularly to condition your mind to achieve the goals. Setting goals is easy, but achieving them takes hard work and dedication. Affirmations, visualization, planning, focus, hard work are all necessary for achieving your goals.

The following affirmations focus on setting and achieving goals. Make them an integral part of your goal setting and achieving program. Select one, two or more GOALS affirmations from those given below and repeat them several times throughout your day, they will provide wonderful results.

Affirmations for setting and achieving goals

- I release all fears of failure
- I write my goals down and review them regularly
- I write down the action steps needed to reach my goals.
- I visualize the achievements of my goals daily
- I write down the action steps needed to reach my goals
- I recognize the barriers to achieving my goals and I move around them, over them and through them.
- I am on the road to success
- I let go of a life without goals and replace it with a destiny of success and grand achieve men
- Everything is working out for my good
- I set and achieve my goals
- I easily reach my goals on time
- I accomplish everything I set out to do
- My goals fit perfectly with all areas of my life
- I enjoy the challenge of my goals
- I easily stay focused on my objectives despite interruptions and distractions.
- I plan my work and I work my plan.
- Each of my goals is assigned a date that I expect to achieve it.

- I have the power to achieve any goal I desire.
- I am improving my attitude
- I now dissolve the habit of putting off difficult tasks

Are you the turtle or the rabbit?
(The turtle going for the win)

We live in a world where everything is instant, Instant emails, text messages, food and instant fame and fortune. Instant mindsets don't see the hard work, dedication, trials and tribulations that got celebrities where they are today. They only see the success.

Instant mindsets only see speed, instant solutions, fast track lives but the people with growth mindsets are the ones who really make it big. They are the ones who know hard work pays off. It may seem slow but it's steady. They understand determination and how to stay loyal to their goals even when it challenging. An instant mindset is not ambitious, and it will never outwork, think or succeed.

The rabbit was caught up in speed (instant mindset) while the turtle was taking his time. Slow but steady (Growth mindset).

Learn patience. Patience is a virtue that will serve you well regardless of your journey and stage in life. If you take your time you will learn more and gain a clearer vision.

You can't rush success by racing to the top. Greatness is not a race, and true greatness is in fact rooted in longevity!

Go for the win!!!

My Testimony Of Growth

I could remember growing up in New Orleans as a teenager. My parents were absent. I was raising my younger siblings and head of my household at the age of 15 years old. My story was filled with hurt, rejection, broken pieces, abandonment, poor decisions, being misunderstood, etc.

However, I always had that self-motivated drive in me, but those feelings I experienced from the pain in my life caused me to wake up on a day to day basis looking for something to go wrong in my life. Sometimes it made me feel like I had no purpose. Instead of looking forward to great things, I would expect the worst. I was here and there. My mind was playing tricks on me.

I was a troubled youth with good intentions. I always wanted better for myself. I was in need of a mentor, mother figure or role model. I have either one. I had to become what I needed for myself. It was challenging, but I survived some of my darkest moments and days. God's word sustained and encourage me. I am living proof that there is a God. Many days I felt like I was losing my mind, but God.

I stand here today as a living witness with a renewed mind and a changed perspective. You have to reset your mind. Say your affirmations and believe them. Pay full attention to the words you speak and repeat. For additional power, write your affirmation down as you speak it in the atmosphere. Say your affirmation out loud in a confident voice several times a day. Say them in the morning, throughout your day and before you go to bed at night. Speak positive affirmations over your own life. Don't speak down on yourself. Encourage yourself. Stop expecting the worst.

Expecting the worst, caused me to walk into fear. It made me feel like I was destined to suffer and that my future held tragedy for me. I had a feeling that I was different and there was something special about me. I had a different glow from my peers. Instead of walking into the fullness of light and letting my light shine, it was dim.

Imagine a dim light in a dark tunnel. That's how I felt most of my days I felt like I was blind folded.

Think about it: when you get up in the morning and you're in a bad mood, worried about something going on in your life, or feeling overwhelmed, those feelings control your behavior, overall performance and anchor you from operating in your purpose.

Q. Why did i expect bad things to happen? A. I expected bad things to happen to me, because bad things did happen to me. Tragedy struck me on different levels, when it struck, felt like I was blind folded, confused, powerless, alone and unable to explain why i encountered those challenges.

I was just a teenager I didn't understand what was going on or why it was happening to me. I knew It was not a good feeling and I had to learn to take control over my own thoughts to change my life. I decide to fight those negative thoughts. I began to grow through the process. Growing through the process allowed me to peek into my purpose.

I gained strength through prayer and Gods' word. My vision got clearer. Along the way god placed people in and out of my life to bless and encourage me.

Illustration: I am like an onion I keep peeling.

The more I peel my life gets better, my mind reshapes, vision gets clearer and I get closer to walking in my purpose. This is an ongoing process. Constantly changing, constantly evolving, constantly getting better.

When my mindset changed, I was able to see and respond on another level. Every mountain I faced and climbed forced me to get to the top. I Climbed it, got through it and around it. After the hardest climb came the peek. Some days I wanted to give up. I had to push through. Those obstacles were opportunities to develop, learn and grow.

It's been a long time coming. Every day I wake up I approach the day on purpose with a positive attitude, saying out loud my affirmations and everything changes. I set the tone for my day. I'm not saying I no longer get those negative thoughts. I'm saying I'm in control. Those negative thoughts get rejected and replace with daily positive affirmations "I am blessed" Today Is another blessed day" I am expecting great things to happen for me. My lenses and perceptions determine the way I respond to situations.

I'm a working progress. You have to put in the work to get results. "The struggle you're in today is developing you to gain the strength you'll need tomorrow. In the middle of every difficult time is a opportunity to grow. The more I grow the more I know. The more I know the more I appreciate and activate in my life.

Your mindsets, thoughts, beliefs, and expectations are the lenses through which you perceive the world. These lenses affect how you live and the choices you make every day.

It's time to reset your mind, make wise choices to constantly grow and heal. Every day is another day to get better, feel better, do better to live better.

How can you heal what you won't confront?

Today is a good day to confront those negative self-thoughts, heal and grow.

One way to confront negative thoughts is to reject them and replace them with thoughts that make you feel better. Let's say you just found out that you have a health issue. You may tell yourself "My life will never be the way it used to be" or "This is the beginning of the end for me." Those negative thoughts will make you feel bad and it will encourage you to give up, just when you need to be strong.

Or you could tell yourself something like "This is going to be a challenge for a while, but if I am patient I can learn to adapt and still enjoy my life" or "This is a setback for me, but I'll shake back and recover from it." This the kind of thoughts that will make you feel better and give you hope.

Having a positive mindset can help your body too.
Do you have any negative thoughts right now? (Sometimes it's difficult to identify those thoughts, to confront.) Take a minute, listen to your thoughts, and see if you do. If you're thoughts make you feel bad or down, remember: You are in charge of what you tell yourself. So, reject those negative thoughts and come up with something that is more encouraging. Encourage yourself, don't tear yourself down.

Sometimes negative thoughts are connected to the way you live from day to day. You may have to switch it up. Here are some things you can do right now to help you shift your perspective to get a better view of life:

- **Focus on what you are feeling right now.** If you're sad, don't tell yourself that you have always felt this way and you will feel sad forever. Sadness passes. A negative thought can follow you forever until you let it go. It's time to flip the script. (say out loud: I am happy, I am excited and outgoing. Today is a great day to smile and be filled with laughter.)

- **Share your feelings with someone you can trust**. Everyone has negative thoughts from time to time. Talking about it with someone else helps you keep those thoughts in perspective.

- **Do something nice for yourself.** Maybe you can take a break and do something that is not harmful that makes you happy.

- **Take time to count your blessings.** There are so many things for each of us to be thankful for. Name a few things you appreciate?

- **Eat healthy. Sleep well. Be active.** The nicer you are to your body, the more you will feel good about yourself.

- **Make social connections.**
  Get up get out and network with others. Fellowship, join a social club, go to the gym. Connect with people that have positive mindsets and can help you improve your life.

If you spend time with people with a positive mindset and consistently making good decisions, our perspective on what "positive" mindset looks like begins to shift.

Surrounding yourself with people that will inspire you to shift your perspective is one of the best ways to put your mindset change effort on autopilot. When negative thoughts are rejected and, in fact, discouraged, suddenly "fitting in with the crowd" involves another level of thinking than what you've been used to doing. Positive thinking will become your new norm.

Positive affirmations will improve your life, build your confidence and will help you develop good habits.

Positive self-love affair is extremely helpful and healthy.

Self-love affirmations is a great tool for feeling better about yourself.

We all felt or feel alone, rejected, hurt or overlooked. Searching for love from others and we forget to love ourselves. Seeking validation and forget to accept ourselves.

I know it's painful when people turn their backs on you or fall out of love with you, but you must continue loving yourself.

Self-love is most important. One minute they love you and the next minute they don't. You have to remember to love yourself.

Before anyone else can love you, you have to learn to love yourself. Maybe you don't realize your lacking self-love. It's time to pay close attention to the way you think about yourself what you say and how you carry yourself.

Below is a list of signs of a lack of self-love. If you exhibit more than 4 of the signs listed below you need to come start working on and building your self love

- Self esteem issues
- Being Needy
- Being withdrawn
- Pretend to be someone else
- Constantly stressed out
- Poor communication
- Hypercritical of yourself and/or others
- Feel untrustworthy
- Lots of self doubt
- Worry more about failures than accomplishments
- Being a follower
- Feel unloved and unlovable

The disconnection from love is the core of almost all our problems. It leads to desperation - imprisoning ourselves, seeking love in all the wrong places, unhealthy relationships, needing love, or caring for others at our own expense.

Lack of self love usually comes from one negative thought. You know that negative thought that says "I am not lovable" "nobody loves me" This is a fear that is not real, but a lot of us believe it. Think it, feel it and act it.

When you lack self-love you start to look outside of yourself for love, hoping to find somebody who can overturn this judgement of yourself.

But the truth is, the only person who can actually change this belief is yourself.

Mindsets matter most. If you are ready to change your mindset, you will change your life. It's a different vibe when you move from self-hate to self-love.

It's time to start loving, accepting and enjoying yourself. Self-love is important, if you're lacking self-love practice using positive affirmations to take with us forever.

It is so important to practice positive self-love affirmations. However, affirmations will build your confidence & create good habits.

Affirmations for self-love

- Today, I choose me
- I choose to love myself
- I am worth
- I am love
- I am growing and learning each and everyday
- I am not my mistakes
- I lovingly embrace all my fears
- I am deserving of happiness, love, peace, freedom, money and anything else I desire
- accept myself unconditionally
- I respect my accomplishments and celebrate my successes
- I am worthy of infinite compassion
- I feel profound empathy and love for others and their own unique paths
- I choose to stop apologizing for being me
- I am at peace with all that has happened in my life
- I am living in peace
- My life is filled with joy
- I am living in abundance

- Happiness flows from me
- I am unique
- I deserve all that is good
- I am healthy
- I reject negative thoughts
- I reject negative self-talk
- I inspire others
- I have a positive attitude

Love and embrace yourself because you are the person, you're going to spend the rest of your life with.

- I radiate and receive love and respect.
- I am loved and respected wherever I go.
- I am unique in my talents and abilities
- I do not need validation from others.
- People see value in my services
- I am rewarded graciously
- I am self-reliant
- I am creative and persistent in whatever I do
- I am grateful for all the wonderful things in my life
- I am full of loving, healthy, positive and prosperous thoughts
- I am unique
- I have big dreams and aspirations
- I do not need to prove myself to anyone.
- I am solution driven. Every problem is a opportunity to grow
- I am never alone in my pursuit of success
- I am not a prisoner of the past
- I have the power to change myself how I see fit
- I am responsible for making my choices and decisions
- I am not selfish
- Every moment brings us a choice and I choose happiness no matter what my circumstances

- I have a growth mindset
- I think positively and expect the best
- I am aware of my strength and act with confidence
- Life is beautiful and rewarding.
- I am blessed
- I am healthy and happy
- I appreciate the things I have
- I rejoice in the love I receive
- I am courageous
- I am hard working and successful
- I am passionate about what I do and that reflects enthusiasm in my work
- I attract positive vibes
- I am open to meeting people and create positive and supportive relationships
- I radiate love and encourage others
- I am calm and peaceful
- I take time to enjoy the little things
- I am in full control of my life

Affirmations to help propel you into success:

- I give myself permission to do what is right for me.
- I overcome fears by following my dreams.
- My mind is full of brilliant ideas.
- I am becoming closer to my true self every day.
- I make a difference in the world simply by existing in it.
- I love my ability to _____
- I give myself space to grow and learn.
- I am always headed in the right direction.
- I now choose to release all hurt and resentment.
- I am the architect of my life; I build its foundation and choose its contents.
- I build up instead of tearing others down.
- I am superior to negative thoughts and low actions.

- I possess the qualities needed to be extremely successful.

- My ability to conquer my challenges is limitless; my potential to succeed is infinite.
- Everything that is happening now is happening for my ultimate good.
- My future is an ideal projection of what I envision now.
- I am love. I am purpose. I was made with divine intention.
- I feed my spirit. I train my body. I focus my mind. It's my time.
- I don't sweat the small stuff.
- I can. I will. End of story.
- I am beautiful inside out.
- I have the power to create change.
- I let go of all that no longer serves me.
- I refuse to give up because I haven't tried all possible ways.
- I deserve the best and I accept the best now.
- It's not their job to like me…it's mine.

Repeat these affirmations as many times as you need to until you are able to let go of the weights you believe you are supposed to hold and refocus on what you desire to. You got this.

What you say and believe matters. You can be your biggest critic, your greatest motivation and your top supporter. Positive affirmations can help you big time. Help YOU convince yourself of your own self-worth.

You have to believe in yourself before you can set a goal. When you believe in yourself it gives you the power to dream big and achieve.

When you believe in yourself, you're not limited to just making it through another day; you expect bigger and better. You are confident and walk by faith knowing you can and will achieve your goals.

Believe in yourself it gives you the power to:

- Love yourself
- Love others
- Overcome negative thoughts
- Set goals
- Dream big
- Push through hard times
- Succeed

I created a list of quotes by some of the world's greatest motivational speakers ever!

The following speakers have motivated millions of people all over the world through their blogs, seminars, videos and books.

If you enjoy reading quotes, I am sure that you will enjoy this powerful collection of quotes.

Take a couple of minutes out of your day to read the list of quotes below to gain enough inspiration to last all week long.

Enjoy the quotes down below, soak in the inspiration and get inspired.

Positive Inspiration Quotes

Positive quotes that will make your day better.

You're not stuck your learning, growing and preparing to blossom.

If you don't love yourself, it's impossible for you to love others or achieve your goals. You can't give away what you don't have. – **Joyce Meyer**

Reset, regroup, refocus, renew and remind yourself that you can do it.
— **Keshawn Harris**
Mistakes are stepping stones to success. They are the path you must take to achieve your dreams.

Low self-esteem is like driving through life with your hand-break on. – **Maxwell Maltz**

You will never completely be free until you fully understand yourself (freedom is within) —**Stephen foucha.... Mr. Round2**

All successful people have a goal. No one can get anywhere unless he knows where he wants to go and what he wants to be or do. "
— **Norman Vincent Peale**

"A goal properly set is halfway reached." —**Zig Ziglar**

"If you set goals and go after them with all the determination you can muster, your gifts will take you places that will amaze you." —
Les Brown

Love yourself unconditionally, just as you love those closest to you despite their faults. — **Les Brown**

"You can do anything if you set goals. " You just have to push yourself "
—**RJ Mitte**

It doesn't matter where you start or where you are right now. It matters where you end. — **Daniel Tapia**

To be yourself in a world that is constantly trying to make you something else is the greatest accomplishment.
– **Ralph Waldo Emerson**

We must fall in love with ourselves. I don't like myself. I'm crazy about myself. – **Mae West**

Accept yourself, love yourself, and keep moving forward. If you want to fly, you have to give up what weighs you down. – **Roy T. Bennett**

If you make friends with yourself you will never be alone. – **Maxwell Maltz**

Happiness is an inside job. Don't assign anyone else that much power over your life. – **Mandy Hale**

The most powerful relationship you will ever have is the relationship with yourself. –**Steve Maraboli**

Respect yourself, love yourself, because there has never been a person like you and there never will be again. – **Osho**

Be your own biggest fan. Love yourself and give yourself the things that you need. – **Mel Robbins**

Don't prove yourself, improve yourself

You can't be what you don't believe and what you can't be what you can't see.
— **Keshawn Harris**

Short inspirational quotes about happiness
The sexiest thing a man can offer his women is a listening ear and his underlying wavering to support. — **Zeeda Michele**

"There are two ways of spreading light: to be the candle or the mirror that reflects it." – **Edith Wharton**

"You do not find the happy life. You make it." – **Camilla Eyring Kimball**

The ultimate measure of a man is not where he stands in moments of comfort and convenience, but where he stands at time of challenges and controversy— **Thomas Harris**

"The most wasted of days is one without laughter." – **E.E. Cummings**

"Stay close to anything that makes you glad you are alive." – **Hafez**

"Make each day your masterpiece." – **John Wooden**

"Happiness often sneaks in through a door you didn't know you left open." – **John Barrymore**

"Happiness is not by chance, but by choice." – **Jim Rohn**

"Life changes very quickly, in a very positive way, if you let it." – **Lindsey Vonn**

"Keep your face to the sunshine and you cannot see a shadow." – **Helen Keller**

Short inspirational quotes about believing in yourself

"Impossible is for the unwilling." – **John Keats**

"No pressure, no diamonds." – **Thomas Carlyle**

"Believe you can and you're halfway there." – **Theodore Roosevelt**

"Failure is the condiment that gives success its flavor." – **Truman Capote**

"It is never too late to be what you might have been." – **George Eliot**

"When you have a dream, you've got to grab it and never let go." – **Carol Burnett**

"You must be the change you wish to see in the world." – **Mahatma Gandhi**

"Stay foolish to stay sane." —**Maxime Lagacé**

"Whatever you are, be a good one." – **Abraham Lincoln**

"You must do the things you think you cannot do." – **Eleanor Roosevelt**

"Wherever you go, go with all your heart." – **Confucius**

"Be faithful to that which exists within yourself." – **André Gide**

"Dream big and dare to fail." – **Norman Vaughan**

"My mission in life is not merely to survive, but to thrive." – **Maya Angelou**

"You are enough just as you are." – **Meghan Markle**

Short inspirational quotes about perseverance

"To be the best, you must be able to handle the worst." – **Wilson Kanadi**

No matter what the situation is. All women know how to do. Is just Do! So keep pushing. — **Mia X**

"No matter what you're going through, there's a light at the end of the tunnel." – **Demi Lovato**

"Life is like riding a bicycle. To keep your balance, you must keep moving." – **Albert Einstein**

"Every moment is a fresh beginning." – **T.S. Eliot**

"No guts, no story." – **Chris Brady**

"Keep going. Be all in." – **Bryan Hutchinson**

"Nothing is impossible. The word itself says "I'm possible!" – **Audrey Hepburn**

"It isn't where you came from. It's where you're going that counts." – **Ella Fitzgerald**

"If it matters to you, you'll find a way." – **Charlie Gilkey**

"Tough times never last, but tough people do." – **Dr. Robert Schuller**

"Turn your wounds into wisdom." – **Oprah Winfrey**

"The journey of a thousand miles begins with a single step." – **Lao Tzu**

"If you're going through hell, keep going." – **Winston Churchill**

"Don't wait, the time will never be just right." – **Napoleon Hill**

"If I cannot do great things, I can do small things in a great way."
– Martin Luther King Jr.

"Life is fragile. We're not guaranteed a tomorrow so give it everything you've got." **– Tim Cook**
"The bad news is time flies. The good news is you're the pilot." – **Michael Altshuler**

Pilots take command. They have a plan, a map and a route. They have the skills and the fuel to get where they want to go. The pilot is responsible and is in control of the plane.

To be a good pilot of yourself, it all starts with you.

Be confident before you take off into your life, dreams and your destiny.

- Be confident
- Be the best pilot you can be
- Be aware of yourself
- Have a good sense of direction
- Be ready before you take off

To achieve your goals, your mindset needs to match your beliefs and aspirations. Otherwise, it might be holding you back from getting where you want to be and making accomplishments in life.

Success and happiness are all about your mindset. Your mindset and belief system affect everything in your life from what you think, to how you may feel and react to situations.

- Determine the mindset you need to achieve your goals.
- Remain a student to learn and apply knowledge.
- Surround yourself with people that match your desired mindset.

- Create new habits that will support your mindset change.

- Get out of your Comfort zone and stay out of your own way.

- Constantly upgrade your mind

- Evaluate your self-talk and the way you talk to other people.

Don't let a negative mindset hold you back from your biggest dreams.

Inspiration Poem

It takes a mighty, strong, & powerful woman to do what you do, up on that prayer line 6:30 a.m. every morning no matter if it's just Jesus and you. You are truly anointed I can feel it in your vibe, the love you have for other's it wears no disguise.
Sista you're blessed it shows up on your skin, you're a beautiful person both outside and in.
A motivator, a teacher, a friend, a leader, rapper and speaker.
I thank God for putting you in my life, your consistency helps hold me together and to do what is right.
I can call you at any given moment anytime,4:00 in the morning, up on the phone crying,you know my trials and my tribulations, your always there when I'm angry and frustrated,
lending me your ear not only that advice and your patience.
Sista you're on FIRE! keep blazing that trail, walking with God everything you touch will continue to excel.
I know, I tell you all the time, but I don't think you understand how proud of you I really am, so Sista do yo thing, go head bring it, stay in the game keep shining, keep winning, it's a uptown thing you know how we finish!
Luv U sis keep up the GOOD WORK!
—By: De'Yanna Brazile aka Doo!

Inspirational Prayer

Dear Lord, I invite you in to begin transforming my thought process and patterns. Help me to recognize and reject negative thoughts and every thought that's not pleasing to you. I long to break free from negative thinking, people and places. Help me to embrace and live in peace, love and joy.

Clear my mind oh lord, help me to overcome my doubts, fear, temptations and of being anxious. Help me to stay focused on you and to allow your word to be activated in my life and my goals. All Honor, Glory and Praise be to Your Name and I love You, in the name of Jesus Christ, Amen

I pray this book motivates to shift your perspective and encourage you to come out braver than you believe, stronger than you seem and smarter than you think…..

Continue to evolve, stay strong and never give up!

EmpowerHer
EmpowerHim

About the Author

Keshawn Harris share her story through music, speaking and writing to inspire others. She is a great inspiration to women, men, girls and boys from all walks of life. She is a rapper, motivational Speaker, Author, mentor, community activist, intercessor, CEO of Making Major Moves, LLC. "MMM" is a branded acronym & hashtag #Making Major Moves.

M.M.M apparel and inspirational T- shirts are available for purchase at (website)

www.iamkeedyblack.bigcartel.com.
Social Media: Instagram / Twitter
Iamkeedyblack
Email: keedyblackbooking@gmail.com

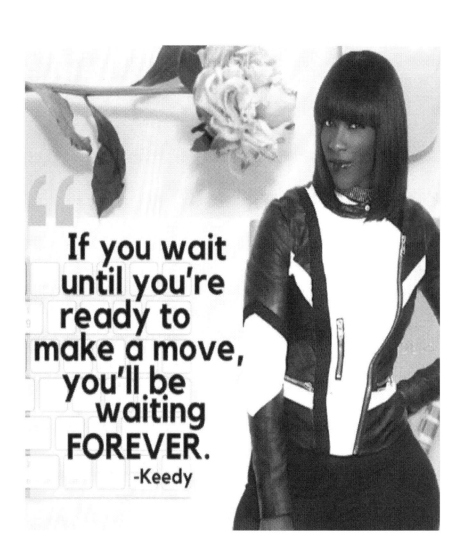

If you wait until you're ready to make a move, you'll be waiting FOREVER.
-Keedy

EMPOWERHER

Made in the USA
Columbia, SC
05 April 2021